THE SINGERS MUSICAL THEATRE ANTHOLOGY

A collection of songs from the musical stage, categorized by voice type. The selections are presented in their authentic settings, excerpted from the original vocal scores.

Compiled and Edited by Richard Walters

ISBN 978-1-4950-1902-9

HAL•LEONARD®
CORPORATION

7777 W. BLUEMOUND RD. P.O. BOX 13819 MILWAUKEE, WI 53213

D1591741

Foreword

The aims of *The Singer's Musical Theatre Anthology* have remained constant since the first volumes were released:

• collecting songs that deeply represent the vast variety in the body of musical theatre literature

• choosing a deliberate mix of contemporary and classic

• categorizing songs by voice type (Soprano, Mezzo-Soprano/Belter, Tenor, Baritone/Bass)

• presenting songs in the most authentic edition possible (which almost always means based on the vocal score, not the vocal selections arrangements which traditionally have the melody in the piano part)

• no repetition of songs from previous volumes (except three very specific cases that are explained in notes in those instances)

• providing information on each show and song so that a singing actor can bring some context to understanding a song

As the curator/editor of the series, I regularly keep notes on what songs from new shows are candidates for inclusion, as well as what classic musical theatre songs have not been used in the series. From these possibilities I choose songs that I think have vocal appeal to a broad variety of talents.

Some songs are easy to classify regarding voice type. Others are trickier. The trend of roles written for a soprano who belts is challenging as to voice type categorization. The many "bari-tenor" songs, straddling the ranges of a high baritone or a tenor, have to be categorized for the purpose of the series. Beyond just range, I consider vocal issues and tessitura, and also vocal color and comfort. In the end, sometimes it's simply a subjective editorial choice as to whether a song lands in the Soprano or Belter volume, or the Tenor or Baritone/Bass volume. Many theatre singers, particularly women, tell me they use both voice type volumes for their gender.

Because there are so many volumes in the series, it is perhaps helpful to know the publishing history of these collections for Soprano, Mezzo-Soprano/Belter, Tenor and Baritone/Bass. *The Singer's Musical Theatre Anthology Volume 1* was released in 1987 and revised in 2000. *Volume 2* was released in 1993; the Soprano and Mezzo-Soprano/Belter volumes were revised in 2000. *Volume 3* was released in 2000. *Volume 4* was released in 2006. *Volume 5* was released in 2008. And now *Volume 6* is being released in 2015. A full index of all the songs in the series may be found at www.halleonard.com. Click on "Vocal," then click on "View Promotions & Teacher Resources."

There are over 1000 musical theatre songs published in *The Singer's Musical Theatre Anthology* series. This vast array allows for many choices, but choose your songs very carefully. Not every song is for every singer, just as not every part is for every actor.

My thanks to assistant editor Joshua Parman for his help in creating *The Singer's Musical Theatre Anthology Volume 6*.

Richard Walters, editor
July, 2015

THE SINGER'S MUSICAL THEATRE ANTHOLOGY
Tenor Volume 6

Contents

ABOUT THE SHOWS

These notes are principally by the editor, at times incorporating writing by Stanley Green, Robert Viagas and others previously published in *The Singer's Musical Theatre Anthology* series and other Hal Leonard publications.

ALADDIN

MUSIC: Alan Menken
LYRICS: Howard Ashman, Tim Rice, and Chad Beguelin
BOOK: Chad Beguelin
DIRECTOR AND CHOREOGRAPHER: Casey Nicholaw
OPENED ON BROADWAY: March 20, 2014

Aladdin is based on the 1992 Disney animated feature of the same name. In addition to songs from the movie, for the stage musical Alan Menken and Chad Beguelin wrote four new songs. The show was first produced in Seattle in 2011, and had subsequent productions before its pre-Broadway run in Toronto. Set in the fictional Middle Eastern city of Agrabah, Aladdin is orphaned and homeless, and survives by stealing food from street vendors. However, he vows to mend his ways at the beginning of the musical to stop being a "worthless street rat" and to make his deceased mother **"Proud of Your Boy."** This is one of three songs with lyrics by Howard Ashman not used in the film but incorporated into the stage musical score. Soon after, Aladdin meets and falls in love with Princess Jasmine, eventually winning her hand and securing a position as heir to the throne with the help of a magic Genie.

BABY

MUSIC: David Shire
LYRICS: Richard Maltby, Jr.
BOOK: Sybille Pearson
DIRECTOR: Richard Maltby, Jr.
OPENED ON BROADWAY: December 4, 1983; a run of 241 performances

Baby tells the story of three couples expecting a baby in different stages of life. Lizzie and Daniel are juniors in college who just recently started living together. Pam becomes pregnant after a long period of having difficulty conceiving with her sports instructor husband Nick. Arlene is a slightly older woman with three grown daughters who considers getting an abortion, while her husband Alan is conversely thrilled at the prospect of a new baby. Danny sings **"I Chose Right"** at the end of Act I. He considers how his life has changed since Lizzie became pregnant and he decided to leave his young single life behind.

BIG FISH

MUSIC AND LYRICS: Andrew Lippa
BOOK: John August
DIRECTOR AND CHOREOGRAPHER: Susan Stroman
OPENED ON BROADWAY: October 6, 2013; a run of 98 performances

The big hearted musical *Big Fish* is based on the original 1998 novel by Daniel Wallace, as well as the 2003 film adaptation of the book written by John August (who also wrote the book for the musical) and directed by Tim Burton. The main characters are Edward Bloom, his wife Sandra and their son William. Edward has spent his life regaling Will with fanciful tales of his past, including a story about a giant fish that jumped into a man's arms after Edward taught the fisherman to catch fish by doing the Alabama Stomp. Scenes jump between the present and the past, interspersed with Edward's fanciful tales. Will and his new wife, Josephine, live in New York City and have recently found out that they are expecting a child. When Will finds out that his future child will be a boy, he vows to improve his relationship with his father as he sings **"Stranger."** Because of Edward's constant storytelling, Will feels that he doesn't truly know his father. Will and his wife travel to Alabama to be with Edward, who has cancer. Will attempts to finally find out what is true and what is fiction in his father's many tales. By Edward's funeral Will has learned that all of his father's tales were in fact based in truth.

THE BRIDGES OF MADISON COUNTY

MUSIC AND LYRICS: Jason Robert Brown
BOOK: Marsha Norman
DIRECTOR: Bartlett Sher
CHOREOGRAPHER: Danny Mefford
OPENED ON BROADWAY: February 18, 2014; a run of 100 performances

The Bridges of Madison County tells the story of an Italian immigrant "war bride," Francesca, on a farm near Winterset, Iowa, in 1965. While her husband and children are away at a 4-H fair, a *National Geographic* photographer, on assignment to shoot the historical covered bridges of the county, knocks on her door asking directions to one of the bridges. The photographer, Robert, and Francesca have an almost immediate connection and they have a brief but intense affair. The musical is based on the 1993 novel of the same name by Robert James Waller. A film version was released in 1995, starring Meryl Streep and Clint Eastwood. After visiting the Roseman Bridge earlier in the day, Robert comes over for a glass of tea and ends up staying as Francesca prepares an Italian meal. Robert leaves so that he can get up early in the morning to photograph the bridge again, and on his way out he sings **"Wondering"** about what their connection might mean. The two share a brief three days together, and Francesca considers leaving her family for him, but ultimately she decides to stay with her husband and children. Many years pass and Francesca's husband has passed away. Though they continued to love one another, Francesca was never again in contact with Robert, who waited for her call for years. He has retired from working due to an illness. He arranges for a letter to Francesca to be sent to her after his death with a picture he took of her on the bridge. He sings **"It All Fades Away,"** as an older man near the end of his life. Robert is a "bari-tenor" role (played by Stephen Pasquale on Broadway), but these songs seem more suited to the tenor volume.

BRING IT ON

MUSIC: Tom Kitt and Lin-Manuel Miranda
LYRICS: Amanda Green and Lin-Manuel Miranda
BOOK: Jeff Whitty
DIRECTOR AND CHOREOGRAPHER: Andy Blankenbuehler
OPENED ON BROADWAY: August 1, 2012; a run of 171 performances

Bring It On the musical was inspired by the 2000 film *Bring It On,* about competitive cheerleading and high school rivalries. The story focuses on Campbell Davis, the captain of suburban Truman High School's cheerleading squad. Campbell recruits a shy freshman, Eva, to the squad. Before summer ends, Campbell finds out she is being redistricted to Jackson High School, an inner-city school that has a dance squad called the Queen Bees of Jackson High, but no cheerleading. Campbell originally wins over the suspicious members of the Queen Bees and goes on to compete against her old cheerleading squad and Eva, who turns out not to be as innocent as she originally seemed. Randall, the school D.J., develops a crush on Campbell and asks her out on a date. She is distraught and angry at herself for lying to the Queen Bees about the prize for the regional competition being college tuition. Randall cheers her up with **"Enjoy the Trip,"** about how to enjoy and make the most of life. Originally a duet with Campbell, the song has been edited as a solo for this volume.

CARRIE

MUSIC: Michael Gore
LYRICS: Dean Pitchford
BOOK: Lawrence D. Cohen
DIRECTOR: Terry Hands
CHOREOGRAPHER: Debbie Allen
OPENED ON BROADWAY: May 12, 1988; a run of 5 performances

Carrie was Stephen King's first published novel, released in 1974. The book was made into a now classic 1976 horror movie starring Sissy Spacek, and featuring John Travolta in one of his first film roles. Lawrence D. Cohen and Michael Gore were inspired to create a musical version of *Carrie* by a 1981 performance of Alban Berg's *Lulu* at the Metropolitan Opera. The musical ran for only five performances before the show's financial backers pulled out due to poor critical reception. In 2012, the revised show was seen in a much better received Off-Broadway production, giving the musical new life in continuing stock and amateur productions. Carrie is an outcast high school student in small-town Maine who has been severely sheltered by her mother, a religious fanatic. As she becomes increasingly frustrated with her situation both at school and at home, she realizes she has telekinetic powers capable of causing severe damage. Carrie's classmate Sue feels bad for the torment that she and her friends have inflicted on Carrie and she convinces her boyfriend to take Carrie to the high school prom to make amends. Carrie accepts, but while Tommy and Sue try to be nice to Carrie, Sue's friend Chris and her boyfriend Billy plan a horrible prank to elect Carrie prom queen and then spill pig's blood on her in front of the entire school. This bloodbath leads to death and destruction at the school's prom as Carrie's anger and powers run out of control. The song **"Dreamer in Disguise"** takes place in Act I. Tommy writes a poem for English class, and Tommy reads (or sings) his poem aloud at the request of his English teacher. Tommy is ridiculed by his classmates for his vulnerability, and Carrie is ridiculed for her heartfelt reaction to the poem, which she says shows that "just because something or somebody seems one way, doesn't mean it is that way."

CATCH ME IF YOU CAN

MUSIC: Marc Shaiman
LYRICS: Scott Wittman and Marc Shaiman
BOOK: Terrence McNally
DIRECTOR: Jack O'Brien
CHOREOGRAPHER: Jerry Mitchell
OPENED ON BROADWAY: April 10, 2011; a run of 166 performances

The plot of the musical *Catch Me If You Can* closely follows that of the 2002 film of the same name, which was based on con artist Frank Abagnale, Jr.'s 1980 autobiography, also titled *Catch Me If You Can*. The musical thus tells the slightly embellished story of Frank Jr.'s life in the 1960s, how he grew up in suburban New York and became a successful con man while still in his teens. Frank Jr. had a traumatizing incident as a teenager in which he walked in on his mother dancing with one of his father's friends. His mom begs him not to tell his father, but soon the two divorce and fight over custody of their son. Frank Jr. sings **"Someone Else's Skin"** as he decides to run away from his dysfunctional home life, turning to writing fake checks to swindle millions of dollars. Abagnale poses as an airline pilot, a doctor, and other professions, and is finally caught by persistent FBI agent Carl Hanratty. The two develop a close relationship as pursuer and pursued. After serving prison time, Hanratty arranges for Frank to work for the FBI on fraud crimes to serve out the rest of his sentence.

ELEGIES

MUSIC AND LYRICS: William Finn
DIRECTOR: Graciela Daniele
OPENED OFF-BROADWAY: March 2, 2003

Elegies is a staged song cycle written by William Finn in the wake of September 11, 2001 which ran Off-Broadway for four weeks in 2003. The songs deal with various topics related to loss, including the death of several of Finn's friends to AIDS and the death of his mother. The last few songs tackle the 2001 attack on the World Trade Center. Like many of the songs in the cycle, **"When the Earth Stopped Turning"** is hopeful and optimistic.

FALSETTOS

MUSIC AND LYRICS: William Finn
BOOK: William Finn and James Lapine
DIRECTOR: James Lapine
OPENED ON BROADWAY: April 29, 1992; a run of 486 performances

Falsettos is set in New York City in the late 1970s and early 1980s. Finn and Lapine wrote three Off-Broadway musicals that are the story of Marvin, his wife Trina, his psychiatrist Mendel, his young son Jason, and his gay lover Whizzer Brown: *In Trousers, March of the Falsettos* and *Falsettoland*. The last two of the trilogy became the two acts of *Falsettos*. Marvin hopes to keep his family unit strong despite the fact that he has left his wife for Whizzer. Mendel, coaching all of the family members through the crisis, falls in love with Trina and the two marry as Marvin and Whizzer's relationship falls apart when the two bicker after a game of chess. After their breakup, Whizzer sings **"The Games I Play,"** as he confronts the painful realization that he does not love Marvin. In Act II, set in 1981 two years after the first act, Marvin and Whizzer are reunited. However, Whizzer soon falls ill with AIDS, and the characters come together around him.

FAR FROM HEAVEN

MUSIC Scott Frankel
LYRICS: Michael Korie
BOOK: Richard Greenberg
DIRECTOR: Michael Greif
CHOREOGRAPHER: Alex Sanchez
OPENED OFF-BROADWAY: June 2, 2013 (closed July 7, 2013)

The musical *Far from Heaven* is based on a 2002 film directed by Todd Haynes and starring Julianne Moore, Dennis Quaid, Dennis Haysberg, and Patricia Clarkson. Set in suburban Connecticut in 1957, Cathy Whitaker is a housewife married to a successful advertising executive, Frank. Their life seems perfect, but she discovers that Frank is a closeted homosexual. As her life and relationship to her husband begins to unravel, Cathy seeks consolation in the friendship of Raymond, an African-American young man who works as her gardener, and causes much gossip in doing so. The story deals with issues of gender roles, sexuality, race and the consequences of social taboos on people's lives in the conservative 1950s. After many bumps in their marriage, Frank breaks down one night and confesses to Cathy that he has fallen in love with a man in **"I Never Knew,"** which destroys her and their marriage. Steven Pasquale played Frank in the limited Off-Broadway run at Playwrights Horizon, a production that was recorded on the cast album, with Kelli O'Hara as Cathy.

FIRST DATE

MUSIC AND LYRICS: Alan Zachary and Michael Weiner
BOOK: Austin Winsberg
DIRECTOR: Bill Berry
CHOREOGRAPHER: Lee A. Wilkins
OPENED ON BROADWAY: August 8, 2013; a run of 174 performances

The musical comedy *First Date* follows the story of a blind date between Casey and Aaron. The two have been set up by Casey's sister Lauren, whose husband works with Aaron. The entire musical, without intermission, consists of the dinner date. Impressions are made and change over the course of the evening, and interludes from friends of the two come in to give their opinions on the date and to provide encouragement. Casey is trying to overcome her love of bad boys who are no good for her, while Aaron is struggling to get over his ex, Allison. Aaron sings **"In Love with You"** after Casey urges him to confront and break up with an imaginary Allison, and he ends up realizing all of the reasons they were wrong for each other. By the end of the night, Casey and Aaron have helped each other overcome their problems and look forward to their next date.

A FUNNY THING HAPPENED ON THE WAY TO THE FORUM

MUSIC AND LYRICS: Stephen Sondheim
BOOK: Burt Shevelove and Larry Gelbart
DIRECTOR: George Abbott
CHOREOGRAPHER: Jack Cole
OPENED ON BROADWAY: May 8, 1962; a run of 964 performances

Full of sight gags, pratfalls, mistaken identity, leggy girls, and other familiar vaudeville ingredients, *A Funny Thing Happened on the Way to the Forum* is a bawdy, farcical, pell-mell musical whose likes had seldom been seen on Broadway when it opened in 1962. Originally intended as a vehicle first for Phil Silvers and then for Milton Berle, *Forum* opened with Zero Mostel as Pseudolus, a slave in ancient Rome, who is forced to go through a series of madcap adventures before being allowed his freedom. The librettists researched all 21 surviving comedies by the Roman playwright Plautus (254–184 BC), then wrote an original book incorporating such typical characters as the conniving servants, the lascivious master, the domineering mistress, the officious warrior, the simple-minded young hero (called Hero), and the senile old man. Both Mostel (as Pseudolus) and Silvers (as Marcus Lycus) were in the rather unsatisfying 1966 United Artists film adaptation, along with Jack Gilford and Buster Keaton. The 1972 Broadway revival starred Phil Silvers. The 1997 Broadway revival starred Nathan Lane as Pseudolus; the role was later played by Whoopi Goldberg. Amidst a knotted, madcap plot Pseudolus has hidden Philia, a young maiden, in Senex's house, but when Senex unexpectedly comes home Pseudolus introduces Philia as the new maid. Hysterium, another slave in the house of Senex, is hysterically alarmed at what is going on, and though in a panic sings **"I'm Calm."**

A GENTLEMAN'S GUIDE TO LOVE AND MURDER

MUSIC: Steven Lutvak
LYRICS: Robert L. Freedman and Steven Lutvak
BOOK: Robert L. Freedman
DIRECTOR: Darko Tresnjak
CHOREOGRAPHER: Peggy Hickey
OPENED ON BROADWAY: November 17, 2013

The musical comedy *A Gentleman's Guide to Love and Murder* is based on the 1907 novel *Israel Rank: The Autobiography of a Criminal* by Roy Horniman. The style of the light hearted musical recalls operetta and the British music hall. The main character is Monty Navarro, a young man in London who grew up in poverty, but is informed following the death of his mother that she was a member of the noble D'Ysquith family, having been disowned after she married below her social class for love. Monty learns that he is ninth in line to be the Earl of Highhurst. After he first writes to Asquith D'Ysquith, Jr., stating who he is and requesting a meeting, D'Ysquith writes back denying his mother's existence. Monty sings **"Foolish to Think,"** about how he won't give up on his dreams of rising above his station. He embarks on an ambitious journey of upward mobility, murdering those relatives who stand in his way in a series of what appear to be freak accidents, such as death by bee sting, a tumble from a tower, or by cannibals in the African jungle. Monty hopes to impress his long-time love interest, Sibella, but she marries another. At the beginning of Act II, Monty and Sibella are still engaging in a secret relationship. He sings **"Sibella"** about his continued affection for her. He eventually becomes engaged to Phoebe D'Ysquith, the sister of a distant cousin who has fallen in love with him. Monty becomes Lord Montague D'Ysquith Navarro, Ninth Earl of Highhurst, but is arrested for the one murder he didn't commit. More plot twists occur before Monty's release from prison at the end of the show.

HONEYMOON IN VEGAS

MUSIC AND LYRICS: Jason Robert Brown
BOOK: Andrew Bergman
DIRECTOR: Gary Griffin
CHOREOGRAPHER: Denis Jones
OPENED ON BROADWAY: January 15, 2015; a run of 93 performances

Honeymoon in Vegas is a musical comedy based on the 1992 movie of the same name which starred Nicolas Cage, Sarah Jessica Parker, and James Caan. The story is of Jack Singer, his girlfriend/fiancé Betsy Nolan, and the wealthy Tommy Korman. Jack and Betsy have been dating for five years. Betsy is ready to get married, and Jack loves Betsy deeply but is troubled by the dying wish of his mother, which was that he would never marry because no woman could ever love him as much as she did. Jack finally decides he is ready, and the two travel to Las Vegas to get married. However, upon arrival the rich gambler Tommy sees Betsy and decides he has to have her. He beats Jack in a fixed game of poker and when Jack can't pay up, he strikes a deal to be able to spend the weekend with Betsy. After being charmed by Tommy, Betsy flies off with him to his vacation home in Hawaii. A cross-pacific adventure ensues as Jack follows hot on their trail to get Betsy back. Jack sings **"Isn't That Enough?"** to his dead mother in Act II, and she finally grants him permission to marry Betsy if he is able to prove himself to "be a man." After some crazy plot twists Jack and Betsy marry in Las Vegas at the end of the show.

IF/THEN

MUSIC: Tom Kitt
LYRICS AND BOOK: Brian Yorkey
DIRECTOR: Michael Greif
CHOREOGRAPHER: Larry Keigwin
OPENED ON BROADWAY: March 30, 2014; a run of 401 performances

If/Then is a contemporary musical that features two parallel hypothetical paths that 40-year-old divorcee Elizabeth's life could take. Elizabeth (played by Idina Menzel, marking her first return to Broadway since *Wicked),* has just moved to New York for a fresh start after a divorce. She meets up with her friends Kate, a lesbian kindergarten teacher, and Lucas, a bisexual community organizer, in Madison Square Park. Kate encourages Elizabeth to become a free spirit, seek out new experiences, and go by the name "Liz." Lucas says she should use "Beth" and focus on her career. The musical then splits off into two possible story lines, one following the life of Liz and the other of Beth. Lucas sings **"You Don't Need to Love Me"** to David near the end of Act I.

THE LAST FIVE YEARS

MUSIC, LYRICS AND BOOK: Jason Robert Brown
DIRECTOR: Daisy Prince
OPENED: 2001, Northlight Theater, Skokie, Illinois
OPENED OFF-BROADWAY: March 3, 2002 (closed May 5, 2002)

The Last Five Years paired writer Jason Robert Brown and director Daisy Prince again after their first collaboration on the revue *Songs for a New World*. This two-person show, which originally starred Norbert Leo Butz and Sherie Rene Scott Off-Broadway, chronicles the beginning, middle, and deterioration of a relationship between a successful writer and a struggling actress. The show's structure is unique. Cathy starts at the end of the relationship, and tells her story backwards, while Jamie starts at the beginning. The only point of intersection is the middle at their engagement. While Jamie's writing career soars, Cathy struggles to make it as an actor and this disparity puts a strain on the couple's relationship. Though it only ran for two months Off-Broadway initially, the musical has become a cultural touchstone of contemporary musical theatre. It returned for an Off-Broadway production in spring of 2013. Jamie sings **"If I Didn't Believe in You"** while in an argument when Cathy refuses to go to a party being thrown by the publishers of his book. A film version of the musical was released in 2015, starring Anna Kendrick and Jeremy Jordan.

THE LITTLE MERMAID

MUSIC: Alan Menken
LYRICS: Howard Ashman and Glenn Slater
BOOK: Doug Wright
DIRECTOR: Francesca Zambello
CHOREOGRAPHER: Stephen Mear
OPENED ON BROADWAY: January 10, 2008; a run of 685 performances

Based on the Hans Christian Andersen tale, *The Little Mermaid* marked the Disney studio's triumphant return to the animated screen musical when it was released in 1989. Ariel, a young, sea-dwelling mermaid, longs to be human. She falls in love with the human prince and, aided by some magic, gets her wish. The phenomenal artistic and commercial success of this film spawned a renaissance of big-budget Disney animated feature films. The film musical of *The Little Mermaid* was adapted for the Broadway stage, with several new songs added, including **"Her Voice."** Eric sings it after he is thrown overboard during a storm in Act I and is saved by Ariel, who swims him safely to shore. Eric vows that he will find this woman who saved his life, though he remembers only her voice and beautiful singing.

A MAN OF NO IMPORTANCE

MUSIC: Stephen Flaherty
LYRICS: Lynn Ahrens
BOOK: Terrence McNally
DIRECTOR: Joe Mantello
CHOREOGRAPHER: Jonathan Butterell
OPENED OFF-BROADWAY: October 10, 2002; a run of 124 performances

A Man of No Importance is based on of the 1994 film of the same name, which starred Albert Finney. The show won the Outer Circle Critics award for Best Off-Broadway Musical. It takes place in Dublin in 1964 and tells of Alfie Byrne, a bus conductor and director of an amateur theatre troupe that has been shut down by Father Kenny, the priest at the church where they rehearse, because he objects to their planned production of Oscar Wilde's *Salome*. Alfie's muse is Wilde, and he quotes him throughout the play. Alfie hides his feelings for the handsome bus driver Robbie Fay, who sings **"The Streets of Dublin"** in Act I. By the end of the show Alfie is able to face himself and who he is as a gay man.

MEMPHIS

MUSIC: David Bryan
LYRICS: Joe DiPietro and David Bryan
BOOK: Joe DiPietro
DIRECTOR: Christopher Ashley
CHOREOGRAPHER: Sergio Trujillo
OPENED ON BROADWAY: October 19, 2009; a run of 1,165 performances

Memphis tells the story of white radio D.J. Huey Calhoun in 1950s segregated Memphis. Huey is harassed for playing black music on white radio stations. His style and the music wins over audiences, however, and he becomes popular. He helps the talented African-American singer Felicia gain a foothold on her career, and also falls in love with her. An interracial relationship such as theirs is unacceptable in Memphis of the era, and leads to Felicia being badly beaten. Huey loses his chance to host a national TV show (à la *American Bandstand*) when he insists on using black dancers. Felicia moves to New York to focus on her career, after explaining to Huey that they could never marry or be together in Memphis. Near the end of the musical, an unemployed and downtrodden Huey sings **"Memphis Lives in Me,"** about his inability to leave his hometown despite the hardships it has caused him.

A NEW BRAIN

MUSIC AND LYRICS: William Finn
BOOK: James Lapine
DIRECTOR AND CHOREOGRAPHER: Graciela Daniele
OPENED OFF-BROADWAY: June 18, 1998; a run of 78 performances

The Off-Broadway musical *A New Brain* was inspired by William Finn's own experiences in 1992 with an arteriovenous malformation that brought him to a near death experience. The musical's protagonist is a songwriter named Gordon. He meets his best friend, Rhoda, for lunch one day and collapses in his food. He is taken to the hospital, informed of his disorder, and told that he needs a lifesaving operation or he might die. The following sequences bounce back in forth between visits by Rhoda, his mother Mimi, and his boyfriend Roger, and hallucinations about his work and personal life. After having a near death experience, he comes to have a new appreciation for his life, his loved ones, and his art. Roger sings **"I'd Rather Be Sailing"** while Gordon is in the hospital, with Gordon adding a duet part at times. The song has been adapted as a solo in the edition printed in this collection. "I'd Rather Be Sailing" could have easily gone in the Baritone/ Bass volume as well, with falsetto singing at the end, but ultimately it seemed more vocally suitable to the Tenor volume.

NEWSIES

MUSIC: Alan Menken
LYRICS: Jack Feldman
BOOK: Harvey Fierstein
DIRECTOR: Jeff Calhoun
CHOREOGRAPHER: Christopher Gattelli
OPENED ON BROADWAY: March 29, 2012; a run of 1,004 performances

Newsies the musical was adapted from the 1992 Disney musical film *Newsies*, which was based on the true story of New York City's 1899 newsboys' strike. Seventeen-year-old Jack Kelly and other paperboys are homeless orphans just scraping by somehow. Jack was previously convicted of stealing and put in a terrible home for juvenile delinquents, but he has escaped. The publisher of the *New York World* raises the cost of newspapers the paperboys have to buy in order to sell them. Jack leads a strike against the *New York World*, helped by his more eloquent friend Davey. During a confrontation with strikebreakers and the police, Jack's disabled friend Crutchie is beaten and taken away to the juvenile center. At the end of Act I an upset Jack sings **"Santa Fe,"** and his dream to get out of the city and lead a freer and better life. The Broadway musical version of the song is quite different from the version in the film (published in *The Singer's Musical Theatre Anthology Baritone Volume 3*). "Santa Fe" is also heard in the Prologue to the stage musical. Jack falls for Katherine, a reporter who covered the strike for a rival paper and who turns out to be daughter of the publisher of the *New York World*. With the support of the governor, Jack strikes a deal with the newspaper that benefits all the newspaper boys, the strike ends, and Jack decides to remain a newsie in New York as he begins a relationship with Katherine.

NEXT TO NORMAL

MUSIC: Tom Kitt
LYRICS AND BOOK: Brian Yorkey
DIRECTOR: Michael Greif
CHOREOGRAPHER: Dontee Kiehn
OPENED ON BROADWAY: April 15, 2009; a run of 733 performances

Next to Normal, which first played Off-Broadway in 2008, is a rock musical that tells the story of the suburban Goodman family, plagued by mother Diana's mental illness and by the haunting presence in her hallucinations of her son, who died in infancy. (It is not until well into Act II that we find out his name was Gabriel.) Diana goes in and out of psychiatric treatment, lovingly supported by her patient husband, Dan. The couple's intelligent and overachieving daughter Natalie is in high school and has difficulty dealing with her chaotic home life. In Act I, Diana seeks treatment from Doctor Madden without the use of drugs, which have desensitized her to feeling anything. However, her dead son as a teenager continues to appear to her in hallucinations, singing **"I'm Alive"** to her as an assertion of his presence. Dan and Natalie fear that the treatment is not working. Near the end of Act I, the teenage figure of the dead son sings **"There's a World"** to Diana, dancing with her and persuading her to come away with him. Diana agrees, only to wake up restrained in the hospital with self-inflicted gashes on her wrists. Though all the family members go through extreme torment, the show ends in a hopeful mood.

ONCE

MUSIC AND LYRICS: Glen Hansard and Markéta Irglová
BOOK: Enda Walsh
DIRECTOR: John Tiffany
OPENED ON BROADWAY: March 18, 2012; a run of 1,168 performances

Once, which first played Off-Broadway in 2011, was adapted from the 2007 film of the same name. The stage musical follows the same basic plot as the film, although it is also quite different from it, with both comedy and sentiment more fully explored in the stage musical. The cast acts as orchestra, playing several instruments, on a simple set that is often the interior of a bar. Mourning a break up with a girlfriend who has moved to New York, a busker (simply named Guy in the script) sings the heart wrenching **"Leave"** on the street in Dublin, accompanying himself on guitar. He puts his guitar in the case and leaves it there. He tells a young Czech woman (simply called Girl in the script) that he is giving up on music because the memories associated with his ex-girlfriend are too painful. She convinces him to continue with music. Over time she encourages him, they form a band together, and he comes back to life. Though they are mutually attracted and have strong feelings for one another, Girl stops any romantic relationship from beginning, as she is married with a daughter. She helps Guy get an appointment with a banker, and Guy convinces him to loan him money to allow him to move to New York and pursue a music career by playing and singing **"Say It to Me Now."** At the end of the show Guy has called his ex-girlfriend in New York, and is moving there, hopeful about giving their relationship another chance. Girl finds a gift from Guy after he leaves, a piano she has wanted with a big red bow on it. *Once* received eight Tony Awards in 2012, including Best Musical. A London production opened in 2013 and ran for two years.

PIPPIN

MUSIC AND LYRICS: Stephen Schwartz
BOOK: Bob O. Hirson and Bob Fosse (uncredited)
DIRECTOR AND CHOREOGRAPHER: Bob Fosse
OPENED ON BROADWAY: October 23, 1972; a run of 1944 performances

Set in the Holy Roman Empire "and thereabouts" in about 780 A.D., the musical uses the historical character Prince Pippin, eldest son of Charlemagne (called King Charles in the show), and the story is of his search for an extraordinary life of meaningful purpose. The show uses the device of a traveling troupe of actors, with the Leading Player as the main figure, and stylized theatrical depictions. Put off by war, Pippin flees to the estate of his exiled grandmother, who urges him to stop worrying and to start living, which means, among other things, enjoying sex. He sings **"With You"** first to one adoring young woman, then another, then another, then a small group of them. By the end of the show, after Pippin has explored various things, he comes to the realization that a simple, ordinary life with one woman is what makes him "trapped, but happy." A 2013 Broadway revival ran for 709 performances.

SWEENEY TODD
The Demon Barber of Fleet Street

MUSIC AND LYRICS: Stephen Sondheim
BOOK: Hugh Wheeler
DIRECTOR: Harold Prince
OPENED ON BROADWAY: March 1, 1979; a run of 557 performances

The fictional story of Sweeney Todd first appeared in uncredited installments in a British magazine in 1846-47. Many versions of it followed in print and on stage. Chrisopher Bond's 1973 play inspired *Sweeney Todd,* possibly the grandest and most operatic musical ever written. Set in Victorian London, in Act I the bill on Pirelli's painted wagon states "Signor Adolfo Pirelli, Haircutter-Barber-Toothpuller to his Royal Majesty the King of Naples." The hardened Benjamin Barker, now calling himself Sweeney Todd, has returned to London to avenge old personal grief after many years in exile on a trumped up charge. He calls Pirelli's elixir piss, causing an uproar among those in the crowd who have purchased it. They demand Pirelli's presence, and he makes a grand entrance. Todd, who wants to start up his own barber business, publicly challenges Pirelli to a shaving contest, with a wager of five pounds. They each summon a volunteer, and the contest begins. The braggart Pirelli goes on and on singing **"The Contest"** while Todd silently waits and in a few seconds performs a perfect shave and wins the contest. Sondheim endorsed this adapted version of "The Contest" as a solo, and even wrote a new last line of lyric for it. *Sweeney Todd* has become a regular presence on the stages of New York and London, and in opera houses around the world. A film version starring Johnny Depp and Helena Bonham-Carter was released in 2007.

THE 25TH ANNUAL
PUTNAM COUNTY SPELLING BEE

MUSIC AND LYRICS: William Finn
BOOK: Rachel Sheinkin
DIRECTOR: James Lapine
CHOREOGRAPHER: Dan Knechtges
OPENED ON BROADWAY: May 2, 2015; a run of 1,136 performances

This musical comedy was based on *C-R-E-P-U-S-C-U-L-E,* an improvisational play by Rebecca Feldman. *The 25th Annual Putnam County Spelling Bee* takes place in the gym of the fictional Putnam Valley Middle School. Six students compete, all with their own eccentricities, along with four volunteers from the audience. Three quirky adults run the competition. Flashbacks for each character, fantasy episodes, and the cast's interactions form most of the comedy in the show. Chip Tolentino is the returning champion, but his pubescent hormones are causing him big distractions. When asked to spell a word he is caught off guard, having been daydreaming about a girl in the audience, which has given him one those involuntary erections common to boys his age. Embarrassed, he does not want to stand up to spell. He finally gives in, but is further titillated by the erotic-sounding word he is given to spell, "tittup." He misspells it and becomes the first student eliminated from the bee, and is then required to sell snacks to the audience. While doing so, Chip explains the reason for his embarrassing early ejection in **"My Unfortunate Erection."**

VIOLET

MUSIC: Jeanine Tesori
LYRICS AND BOOK: Brian Crawley
DIRECTOR: Leigh Silverman
CHOREOGRAPHER: Jeffrey Page
OPENED OFF-BROADWAY: March 11, 1997 (closed April 6, 1997)
OPENED ON BROADWAY: April 20, 2014; a run of 128 performances

Violet is based on the Doris Betts short story "The Ugliest Pilgrim." Set in 1964, Violet is a young woman who was facially disfigured in an accident as a child. She travels by bus from Spruce Pine, North Carolina, to Tulsa, Oklahoma, where she hopes to be healed by a televangelist. On the way we learn of her story as she talks with fellow travelers, and her father is seen in flashbacks. She meets a black sergeant named Flick and a white corporal and paratrooper named Monty, both on their way to Fort Smith, Arkansas. The three become friends, with both developing romantic feelings for Violet. Flick encourages her to be strong and fine on her own without the help of a preacher in **"Let It Sing."** At a stopover at a boarding house in Memphis Monty has entered Violet's room while she sleeps. She wakes and asks him to explain himself, and he sings **"Last Time I Came to Memphis."** (This song was sung here in the 2014 Broadway production. In the original version of the show "You're Different" is sung here.) For a time after visiting the Tulsa preacher Violet believes a miracle has happened, but she later realizes that though nothing about her has changed physically, she has changed and has emotionally healed, and upon meeting Flick again, takes his hand to start a life together. Sutton Foster played the title role in a limited Broadway run in 2014.

WONDERLAND

MUSIC: Frank Wildhorn
LYRICS: Jack Murphy
BOOK: Gregory Boyd
DIRECTOR: Gregory Boyd
CHOREOGRAPHER: Marguerite Derricks
OPENED ON BROADWAY: April 17, 2011; a run of 33 performances

This contemporary retelling of Lewis Carroll's *Alice's Adventures in Wonderland* and *Through the Looking-Glass* takes place in modern day New York City. Writer Alice Cornwinkle is taking a break from her husband, wanting some time on her own, and moved with her 10-year-old daughter Chloe to a new apartment in Queens. Alice, having a terrible day, hits Chloe in a service elevator and then receives news that her most recent children's book has been rejected by a publisher for being "too dark." When she subsequently lies down and falls asleep, she awakens to find a white rabbit, with whom she travels down a rabbit hole to Wonderland. All of the classic characters from the books make an appearance, such as the Caterpillar, Mad Hatter, Cheshire Cat, and the Queen of Hearts. In Act I Alice encounters the White Knight (a depiction of a chess piece in the books), who makes an elaborate entrance. He swears to protect and save Alice, with his cronies as his backup singers, in **"One Knight."** To Alice he represents her "hero," her husband Jack.

PROUD OF YOUR BOY

from *Aladdin*

Music by ALAN MENKEN
Lyrics by HOWARD ASHMAN

With determination, poco rubato

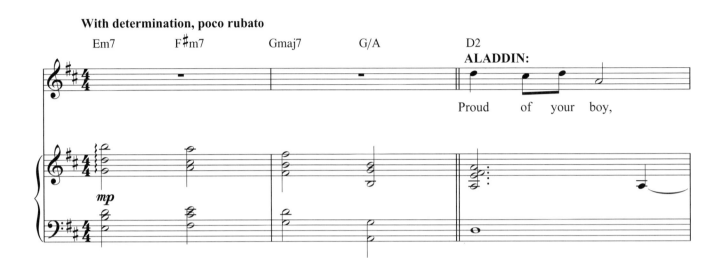

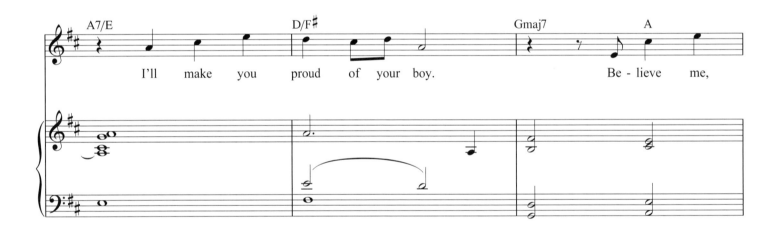

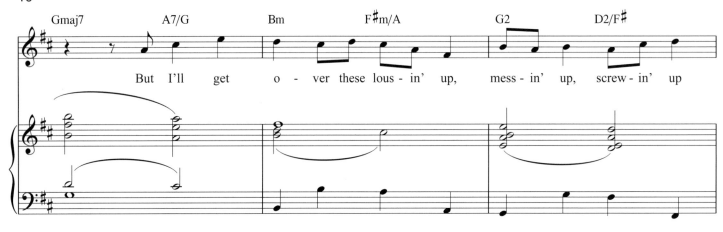

But I'll get o - ver these lous - in' up, mess - in' up, screw - in' up

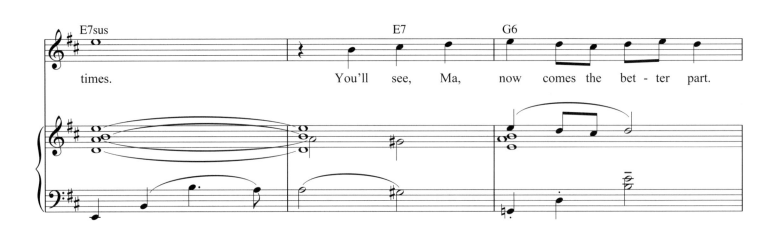

times. You'll see, Ma, now comes the bet - ter part.

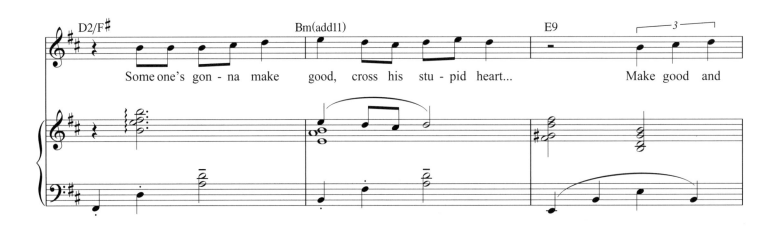

Some one's gon - na make good, cross his stu - pid heart... Make good and

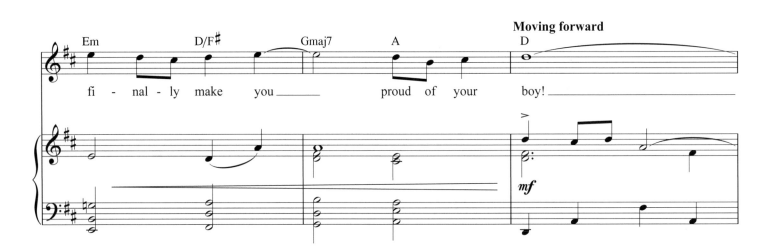

fi - nal - ly make you proud of your boy!

I CHOSE RIGHT

from the Musical *Baby*

Lyrics by RICHARD MALTBY, JR.
Music by DAVID SHIRE

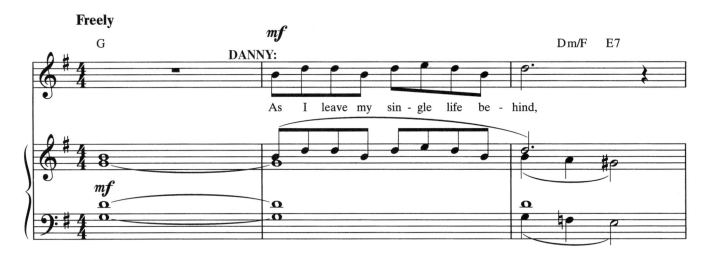

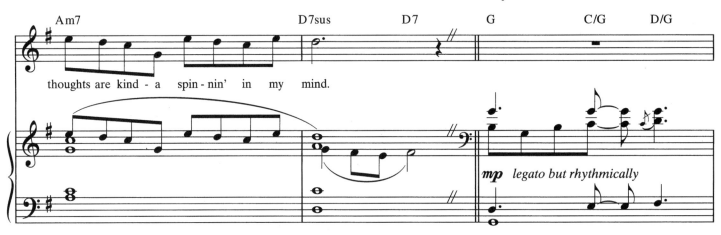

STRANGER
from *Big Fish*

Music and Lyrics by
ANDREW LIPPA

28

when he's born,_ I'll teach him how_ to use____ his com - mon sense._ He'll

lis - ten and__ he'll learn_ and he'll_ ex - cel.____ I'll

tell my son_ that life is lived_ in clear and pres -ent tense,_ not on -

- ly in___ the sto - ries we__ can tell.____ My

father told me stories I could never comprehend.____ In

every tale__ he'd claim__ to be__ the hero._____ I've

Broadly

tried to understand__ him,__ but I wonder if I__ can. Because after almost thirty years, __ I

a tempo

still don't know the man._____ I

WONDERING
from *The Bridges of Madison County*

Music and Lyrics by
JASON ROBERT BROWN

Moderato, with stillness (♩= 112)

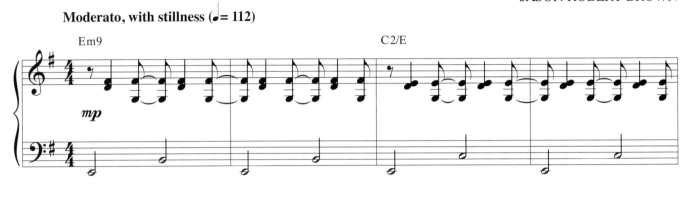

ROBERT:

A lit-tle twinge,__ A lit-tle shock,__ A lit-tle whis-per at the bot-tom of __ your mem-ory.

A sud-den wind__ A gen-tle knock,__ And then a rus-tle____ in

42

IT ALL FADES AWAY
from *The Bridges of Madison County*

Music and Lyrics by
JASON ROBERT BROWN

Freely

There was some-thing in a des-ert.___ There was some-place wild and green, And a

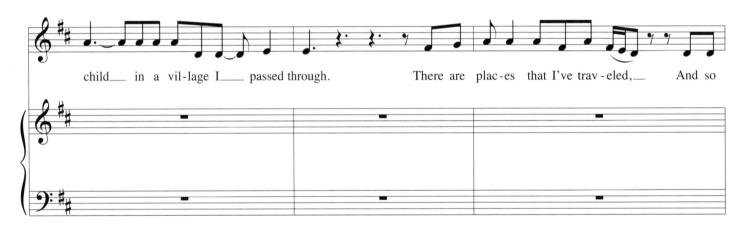

child___ in a vil-lage I___ passed through. There are plac-es that I've trav-eled,___ And so

man-y things___ I've seen, And___ it all fades a-way___ but

ENJOY THE TRIP
from *Bring It On*

Music by TOM KITT
Lyrics by AMANDA GREEN

Driving mid-tempo Pop (♩ = 83)

RANDALL:

I'm a

stud now, __ it's clear so it'-ll shock you __ to hear __ that

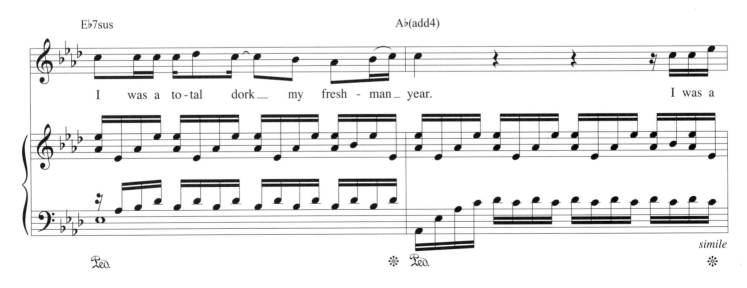

I was a to-tal dork __ my fresh-man __ year. I was a

(guitar strum)

DREAMER IN DISGUISE
from *Carrie the Musical*

Music by MICHAEL GORE
Lyrics by DEAN PITCHFORD

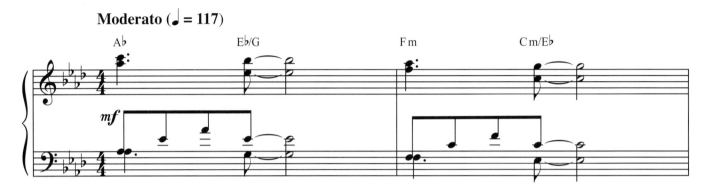

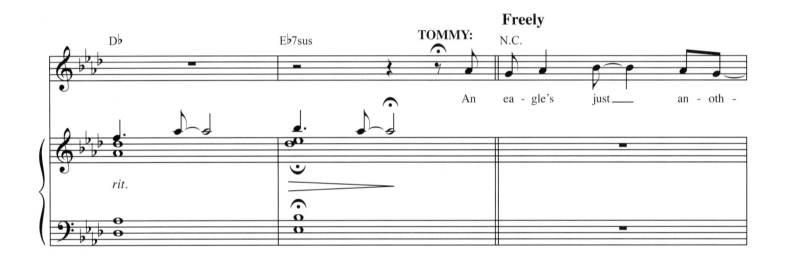

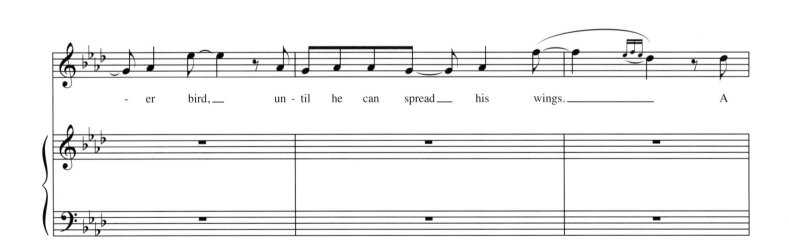

SOMEONE ELSE'S SKIN

from *Catch Me If You Can*

Lyrics by SCOTT WITTMAN and MARC SHAIMAN
Music by MARC SHAIMAN

Judge: Son, listen to me. We just need a name; your mother or your father.

Judge: It can get very expensive, people fighting over their children.

* The spoken lines may be omitted for a solo performance.

WHEN THE EARTH STOPPED TURNING

from *Elegies*

Words and Music by
WILLIAM FINN

78

80

THE GAMES I PLAY

from *Falsettos*

Words and Music by
WILLIAM FINN

Slowly (♩ = 69)

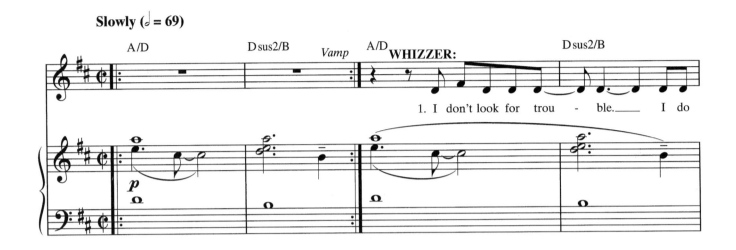

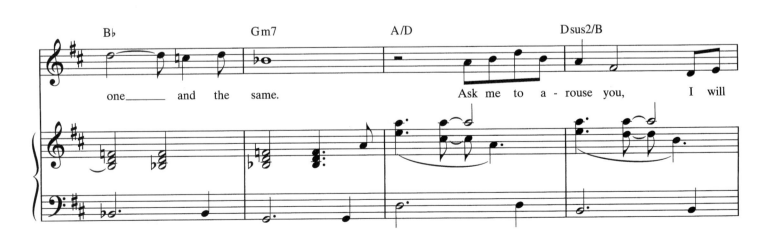

I NEVER KNEW

from *Far from Heaven*

Music by SCOTT FRANKEL
Lyrics by MICHAEL KORIE

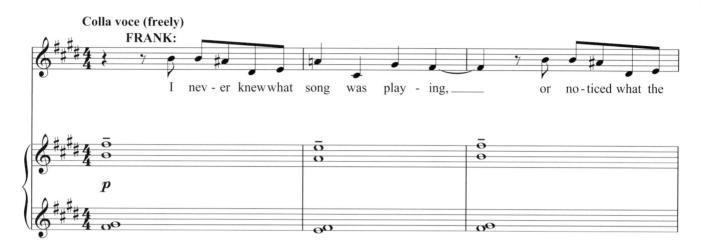

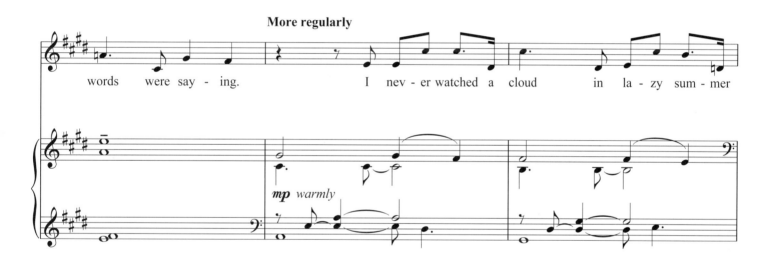

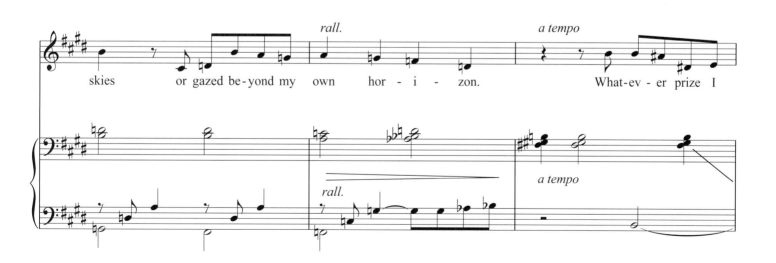

94

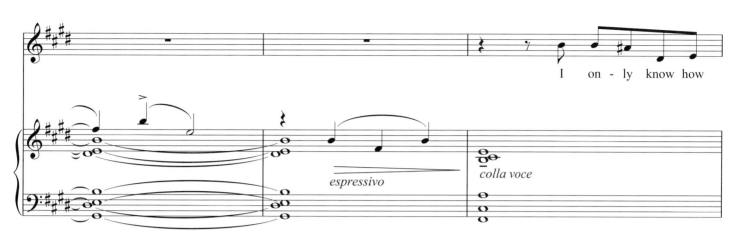

I on - ly know how

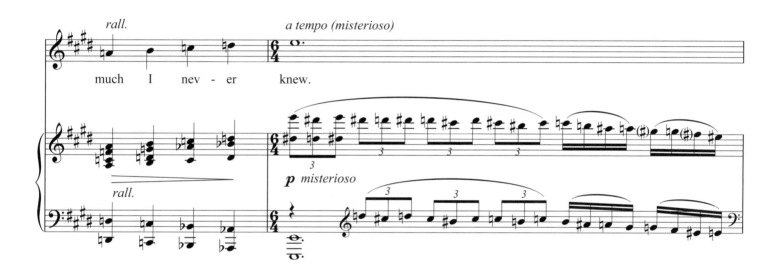

much I nev - er knew.

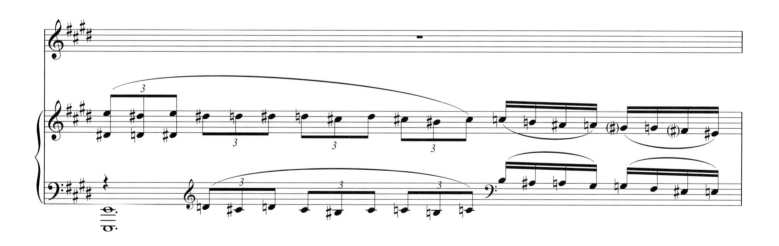

IN LOVE WITH YOU
from the Musical *First Date*

Music and Lyrics by
ALAN ZACHARY and MICHAEL WEINER

ISN'T THAT ENOUGH
from *Honeymoon in Vegas*

Music and Lyrics by
JASON ROBERT BROWN

cor - ner, I'm off the fence. She makes my whole world make sense, and

Ma - ma, that's e - nough.

Ma - ma, that's e - nough for me.

I'M CALM
from *A Funny Thing Happened on the Way to the Forum*

Words and Music by
STEPHEN SONDHEIM

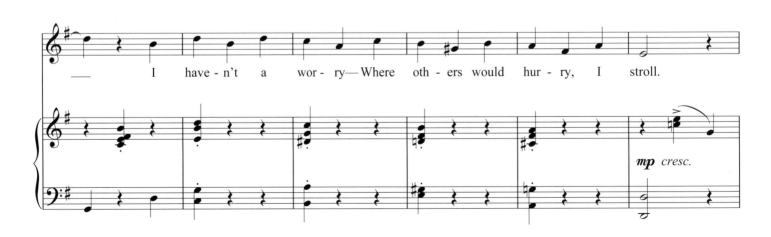

(He walks around rapidly)

I'm

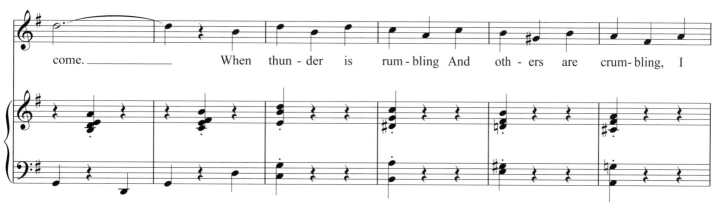

calm, I'm cool, A gib - ber - ing fool Is some - thing I nev - er be -

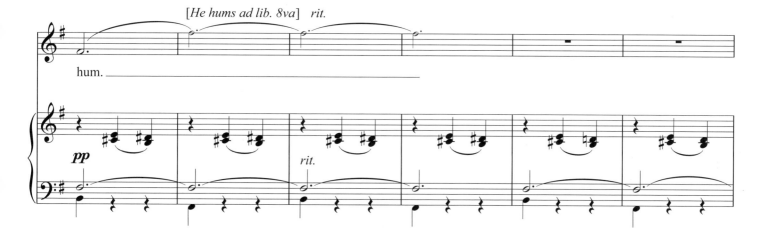

come. _____ When thun - der is rum - bling And oth - ers are crum - bling, I

[He hums ad lib. 8va] *rit.*

hum. _____

FOOLISH TO THINK
from *A Gentleman's Guide to Love and Murder*

Music by STEVEN LUTVAK
Lyrics by ROBERT L. FREEDMAN and
STEVEN LUTVAK

120

* Measures 86–101 were cut for the Broadway production. Cut to **

SIBELLA
from *A Gentleman's Guide to Love and Murder*

Music by STEVEN LUTVAK
Lyrics by ROBERT L. FREEDMAN and
STEVEN LUTVAK

Molto rubato

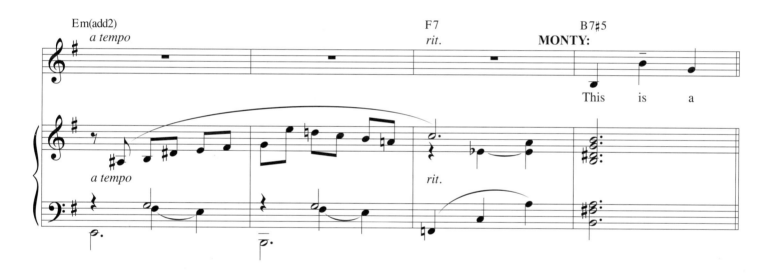

MONTY: This is a

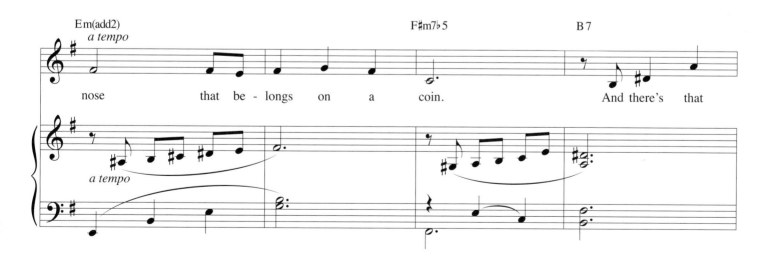

nose that be-longs on a coin. And there's that

130

And I want you that

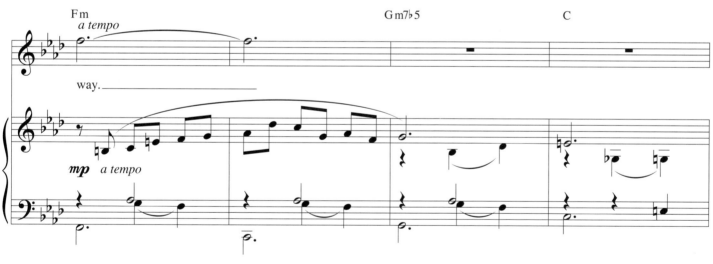

way.

YOU DON'T NEED TO LOVE ME

from *If/Then*

Lyrics by BRIAN YORKEY
Music by TOM KITT

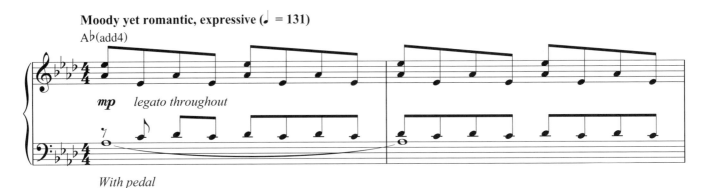

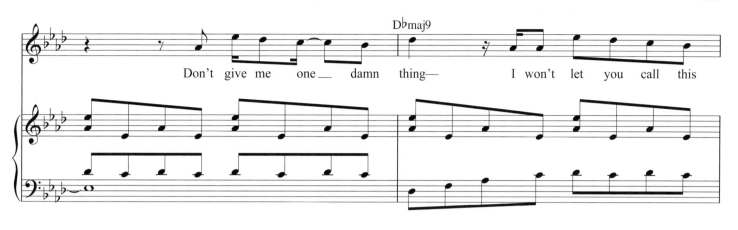

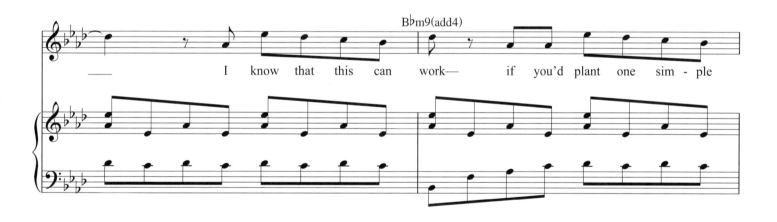

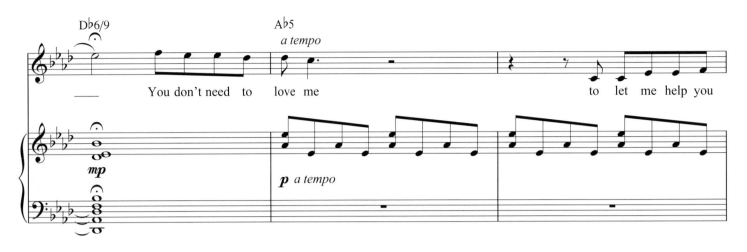

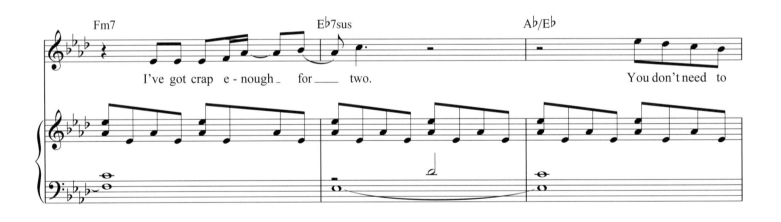

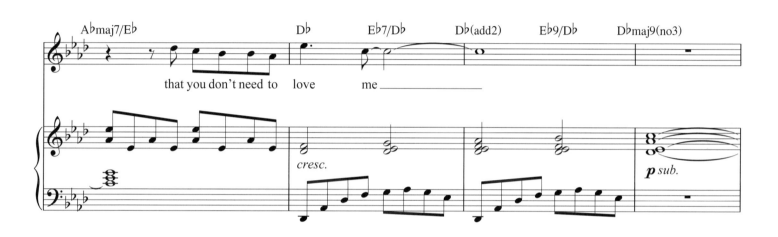

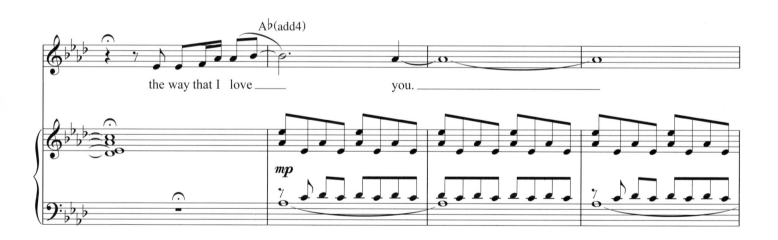

HER VOICE
from Walt Disney's *The Little Mermaid - A Broadway Musical*

Music by ALAN MENKEN
Lyrics by GLENN SLATER

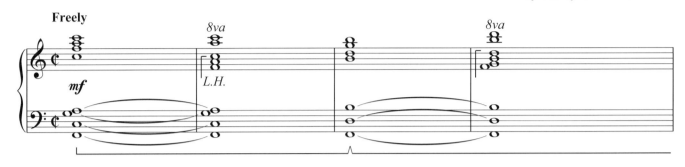

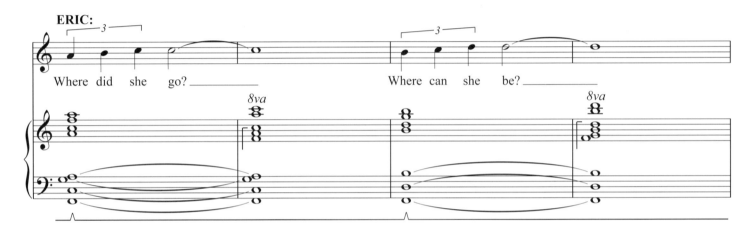

Where did she go? Where can she be?

When will she come a-gain, call-ing to me, call-ing to

me, call-ing to me?

Some-where there's a girl who's like the shim-mer of the wind up-on the

wa - ter.

Some-where there's a girl who's like the

glim-mer of the sun-light on the sea.

Some-where there's a girl who's like a swell of end-less mu - sic.

Some-where she is sing-ing and her song is meant for me. ____ And her voice, it's sweet as an-gels sigh - ing. ____ And her voice, it's warm as sum-mer sky. ____

And that sound, it haunts my dreams and spins me 'round un - til it seems I'm fly - ing, her voice.

mp

I can sense her laugh-ter in the

THE STREETS OF DUBLIN
from *A Man of No Importance*

Words by LYNN AHRENS
Music by STEPHEN FLAHERTY

153

IF I DIDN'T BELIEVE IN YOU

from *The Last Five Years*

Music and Lyrics by
JASON ROBERT BROWN

The first vocal note is played three times on accompaniment recording so that singer may get pitch.

166

MEMPHIS LIVES IN ME

from *Memphis*

Music by DAVID BRYAN
Lyrics by JOE DiPIETRO and DAVID BRYAN

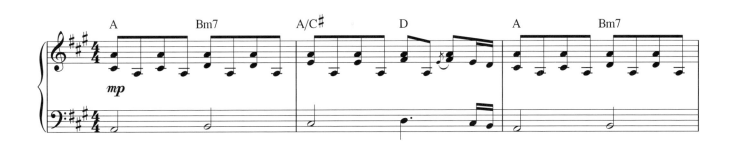

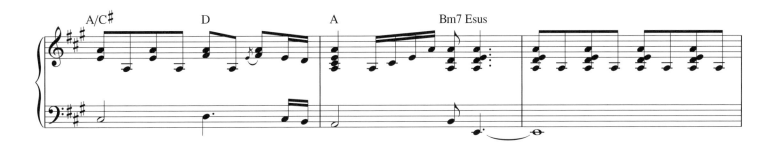

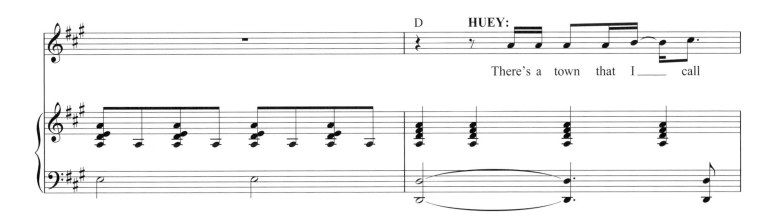

The ensemble parts have been eliminated for this solo version.

170

I'D RATHER BE SAILING

from *A New Brain*

Words and Music by
WILLIAM FINN

Gordo joins for a duet briefly in the middle of the song, eliminated in this solo version.

SANTA FE
from Walt Disney's *Newsies*
(Broadway Version)

Music by ALAN MENKEN
Lyrics by JACK FELDMAN

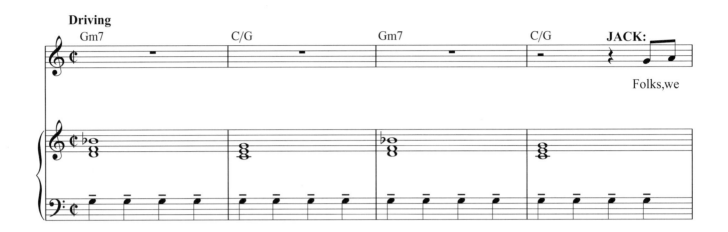

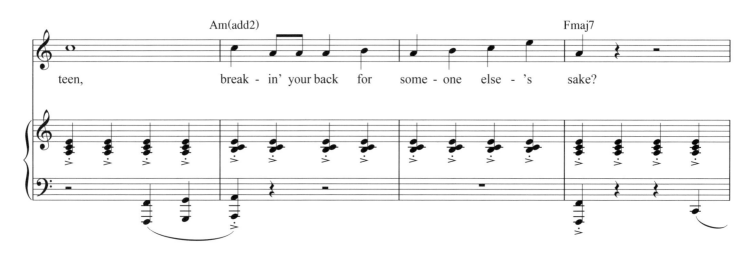

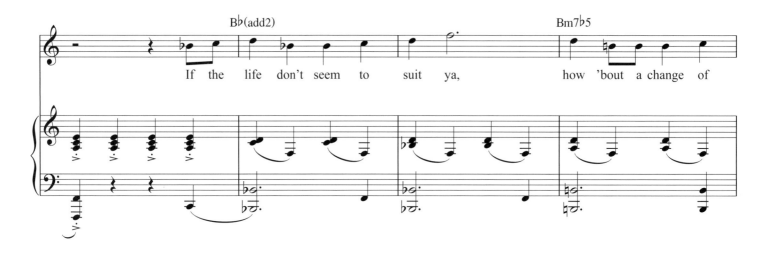

I'M ALIVE
from *Next to Normal*

Lyrics by BRIAN YORKEY
Music by TOM KITT

Moderately bright rock ♩ = 160

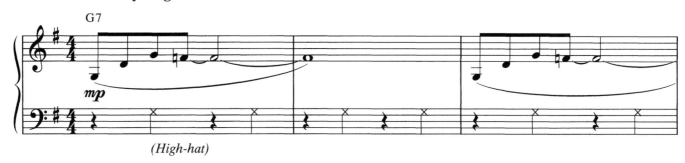

(High-hat)

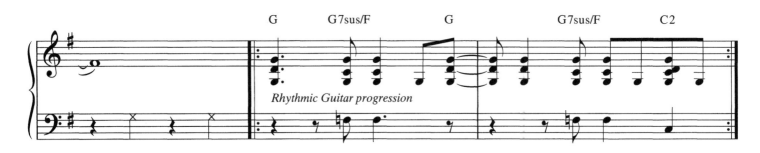

Rhythmic Guitar progression

GABE:

I am what you want____ me to be, and I'm your____ worst fear,____ you'll find____

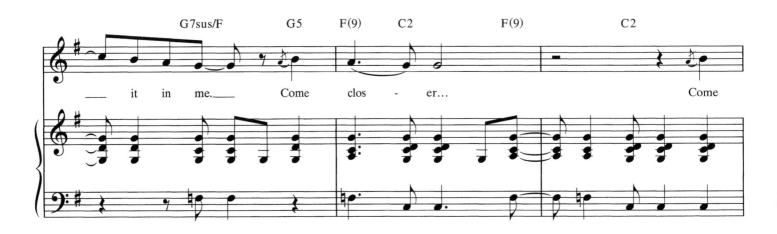

____ it in me.____ Come clos - er... Come

192

THERE'S A WORLD

from *Next to Normal*

Lyrics by BRIAN YORKEY
Music by TOM KITT

THE CONTEST

from *Sweeney Todd*

Words and Music by
STEPHEN SONDHEIM

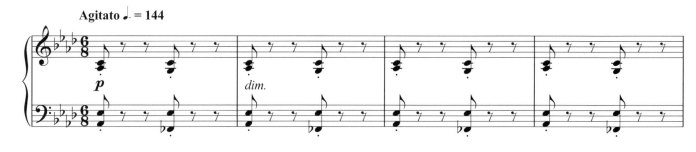

The stage directions for the shaving contest with Todd are preserved for the singer's comprehension; they are not recommended for a stand-alone, concert performance of the song. The piece has been slightly adapted for this edition. The final line of the lyric was written by the composer especially for this edition.

as he accidentally lathers his nose)

beg - a your par - don— 'll prob - a - bly say it was on - ly a car - di - nal.

(Finishes lathering the man)

Meno mosso, molto rubato

(Exchanges his brush for a razor)

mp

Nope! It was - a da Pope! To shave - a da

mf *f*

(Shaves his man, with flourishes)
grazioso

face, To pull - a - da toot' Re - qui - re da grace And not - a da

mp

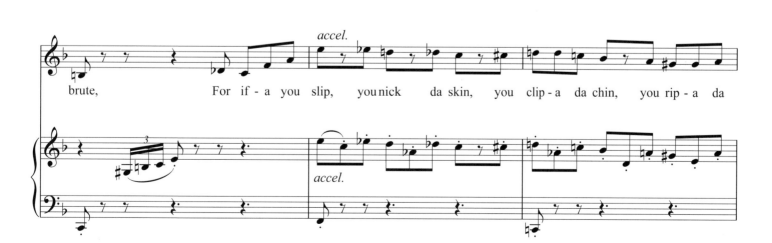

accel.

brute, For if - a you slip, you nick da skin, you clip - a da chin, you rip - a da

accel.

LEAVE
from the Broadway Musical *Once*

Words and Music by
GLEN HANSARD

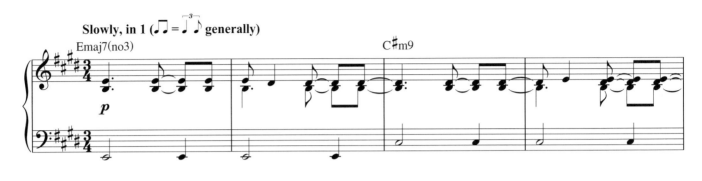

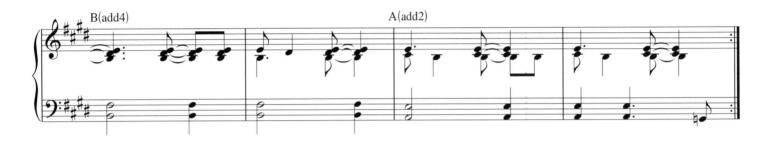

"I can't wait for - ev - er,"
And I hope you feel bet - ter, is

all that you said __
now that it's out. __

be - fore you stood up.
What took you so long? __

This edition is based on the Broadway original cast recording. The piano part is an idiomatic arrangement for the instrument in the spirit of the cast recording guitar accompaniment.

209

*Pronounced "eye"

SAY IT TO ME NOW
from the Broadway Musical *Once*

Words and Music by GLEN HANSARD,
GRAHAM DOWNEY, PAUL BRENNAN,
NOREEN O'DONNELL, COLM MACCONIOMAIRE
and DAVID ODLUM

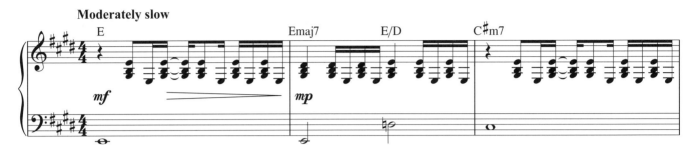

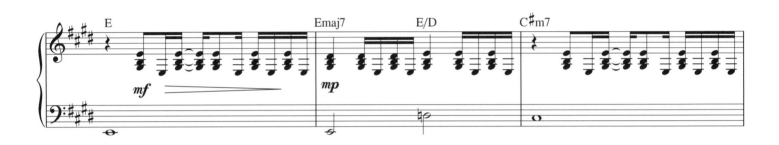

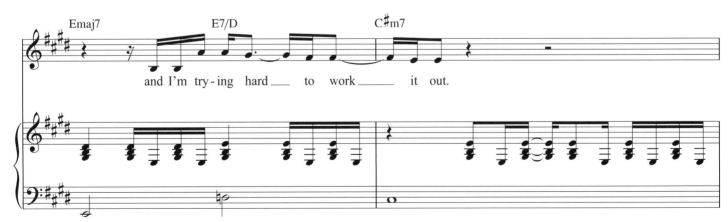

This edition is based on the Broadway original cast recording. The piano part is an idiomatic arrangement for the instrument in the spirit of the cast recording guitar accompaniment.

WITH YOU
from *Pippin*

Words and Music by
STEPHEN SCHWARTZ

tru - ly be - gun. And time weaves rib-bons of mem-o-ry _____

to sweet-en life when youth is through. But I would need no

mem - 'ries there _ if I could share my _ life _____ with _

you. _____

MY UNFORTUNATE ERECTION

from *The 25th Annual Putnam County Spelling Bee*

Words and Music by
WILLIAM FINN

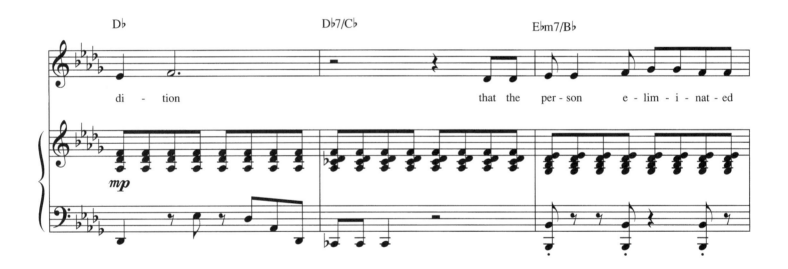

222

LET IT SING
from *Violet*

Music by JEANINE TESORI
Lyrics by BRIAN CRAWLEY

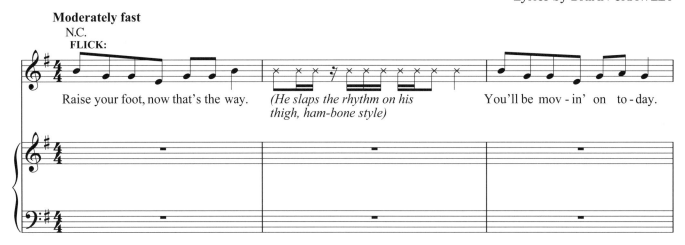

Raise your foot, now that's the way. *(He slaps the rhythm on his thigh, ham-bone style)* You'll be mov - in' on to - day.

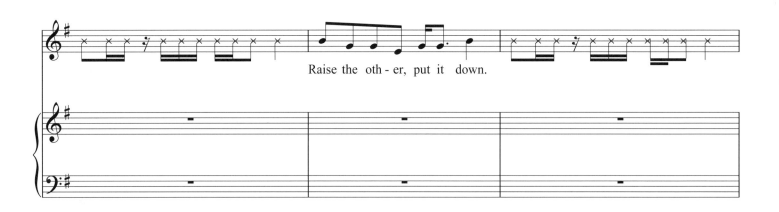

Raise the oth - er, put it down.

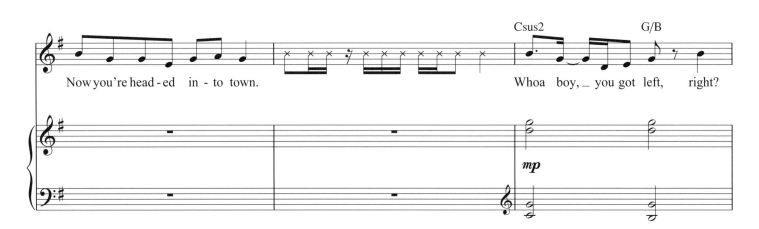

Now you're head - ed in - to town. Whoa boy, __ you got left, right?

Oh boy, __ ain't that __ right? _____ Got some years a - head __ to go.

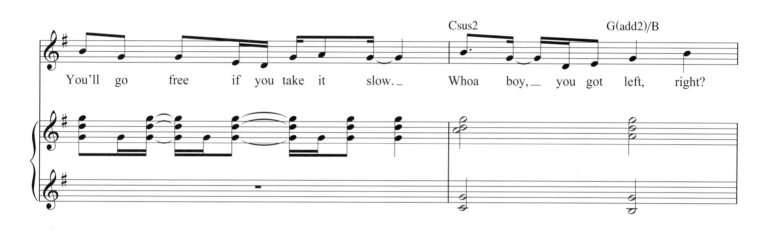

You'll go free if you take it slow. _ Whoa boy, __ you got left, right?

Oh boy, __ ain't that __ right? _____ Two kinds of peo-ple in ___ this

world: some say yes __ and some __ say no. Time to say __ what side you're on,

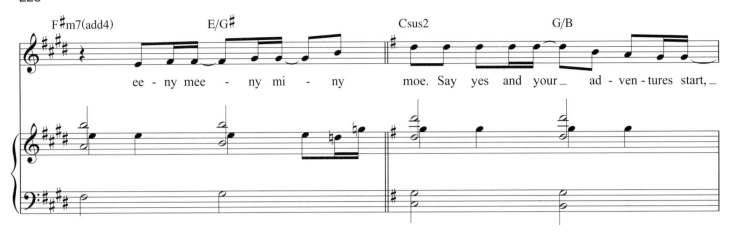

eeny mee - ny mi - ny moe. Say yes and your_ ad - ven - tures start,_

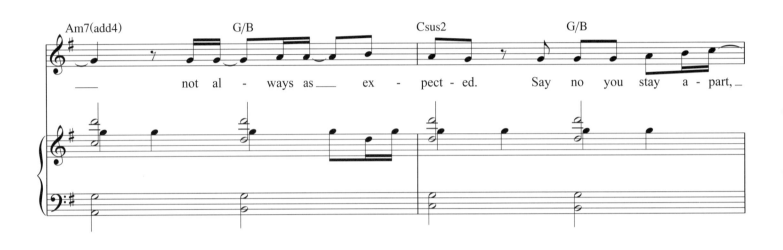

_ not al - ways as_ ex - pect - ed. Say no you stay a - part,_

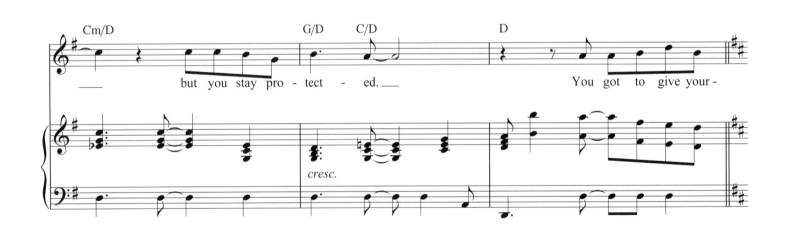

_ but you stay pro - tect - ed._ You got to give your-

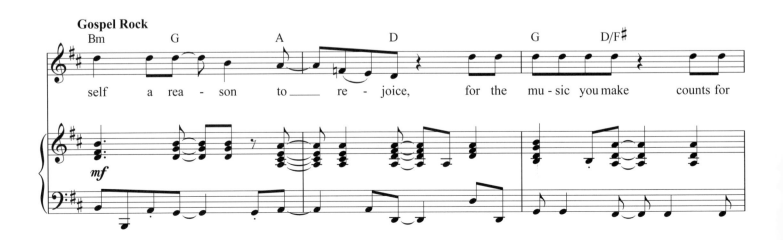

self a rea - son to_ re - joice, for the mu - sic you make counts for

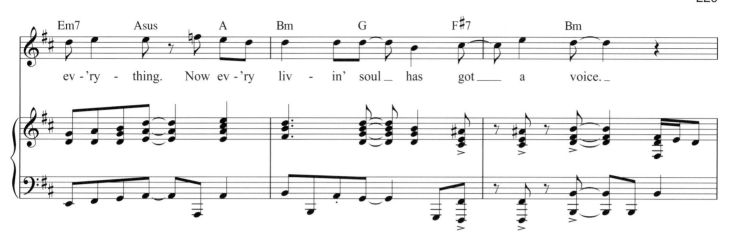

ev -'ry - thing. Now ev -'ry liv - in' soul __ has got __ a voice. __

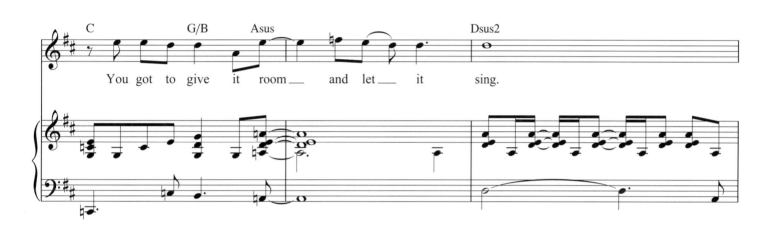

You got to give it room __ and let __ it sing.

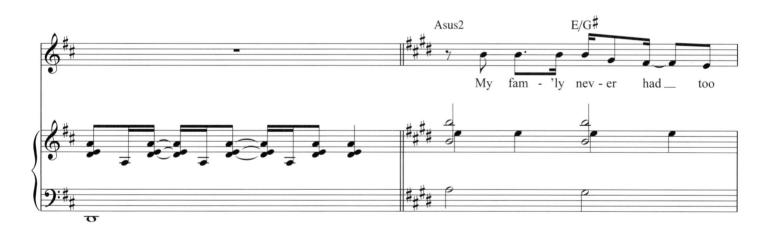

My fam - 'ly nev - er had __ too

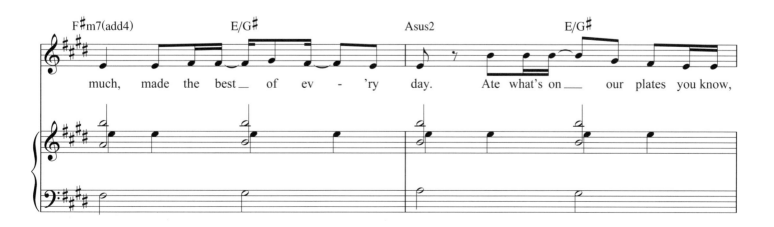

much, made the best __ of ev - 'ry day. Ate what's on __ our plates you know,

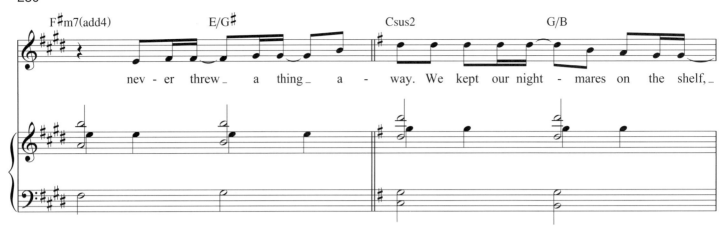

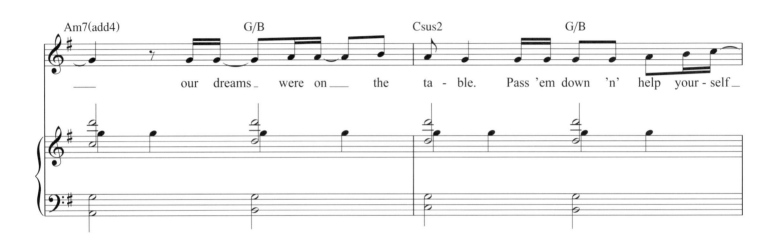

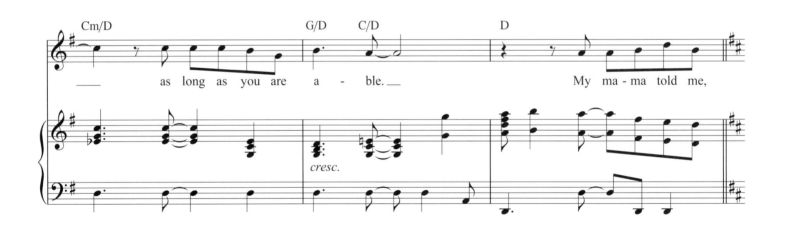

LAST TIME I CAME TO MEMPHIS

from *Violet*

Music by JEANINE TESORI
Lyrics by BRIAN CRAWLEY

ONE KNIGHT
from the Broadway Musical *Wonderland*

Music by FRANK WILDHORN
Lyrics by JACK MURPHY

The ensemble background harmonies may be omitted for a solo performance.
This is the original key from the piano/conductor rehearsal score, and the key of performance on Broadway in 2011. On the 2009 cast recording, the song is one whole step higher.

throw in a la-dy if you can. Though I'm not Lan-ce-lot, I'll be brav - er.

Ooh, ooh, lot, I'll be brav - er.

I'll rush in ___ to save ___ the day. It -'ll look ___ good on ___ my

I'll _____ save _ the day. ___

ré-su-mé. ___ I don't care ___ a - bout ___ the take - home pay. I just wan-

Ré-su-mé. ___ take - home pay. ___

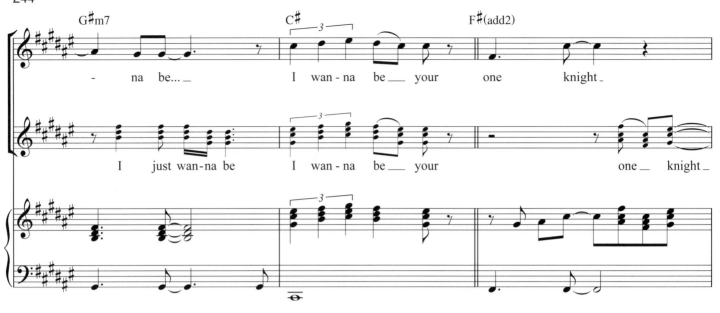

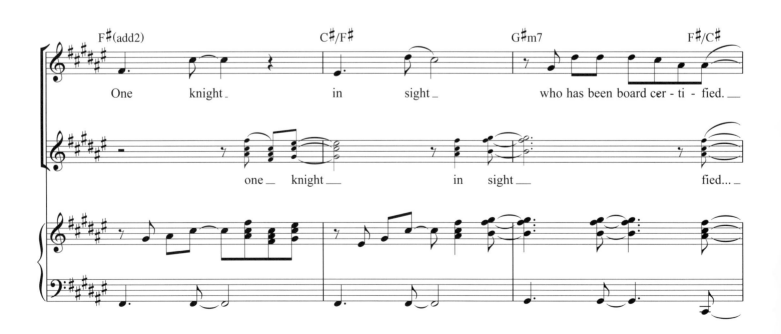

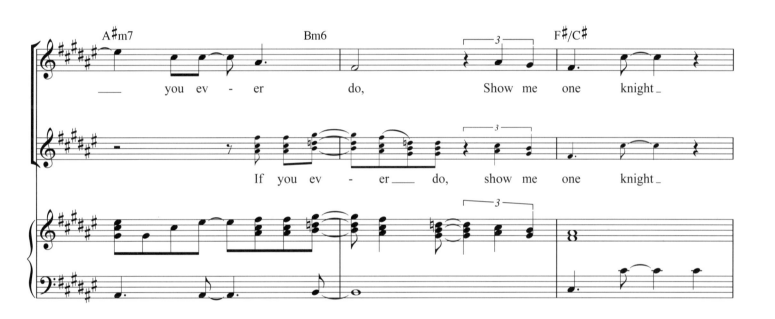

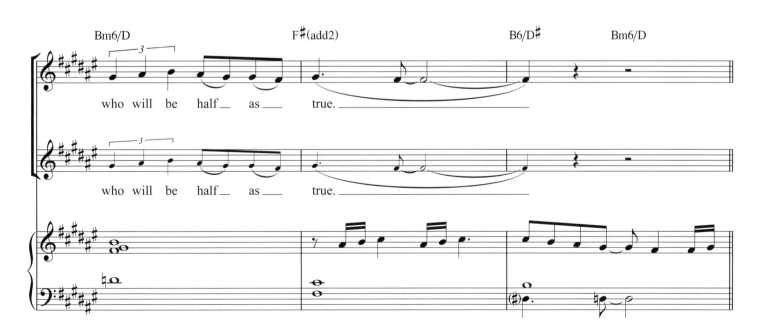

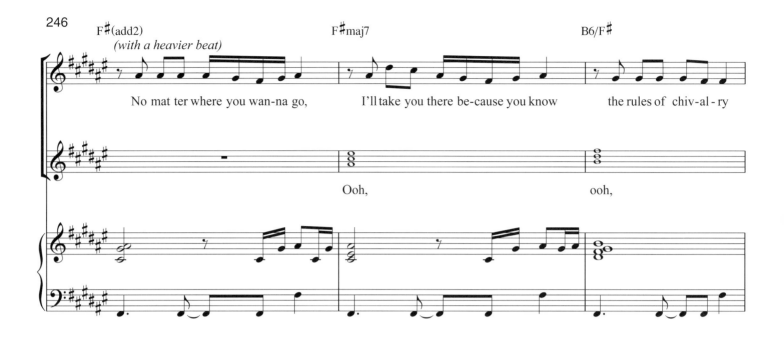

No mat-ter where you wan-na go, I'll take you there be-cause you know the rules of chiv-al-ry

Ooh, ooh,

are-n't quite dead yet. So if you stick a-round with me, I prom-ise you you're gon-na see

are-n't quite dead yet. ___ Ooh,

a hap-py end-ing rid-ing in-to the sun-set. When there is ___ a real ___

ooh, in-to the sun-set. Ah, ___

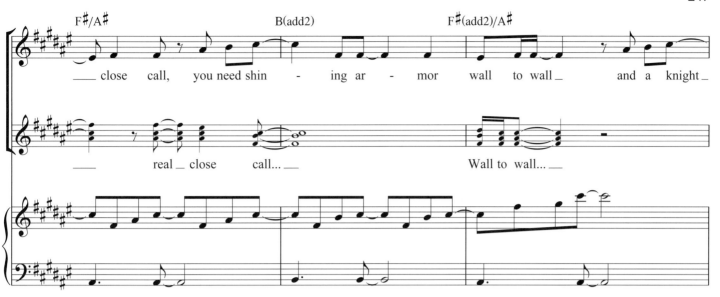

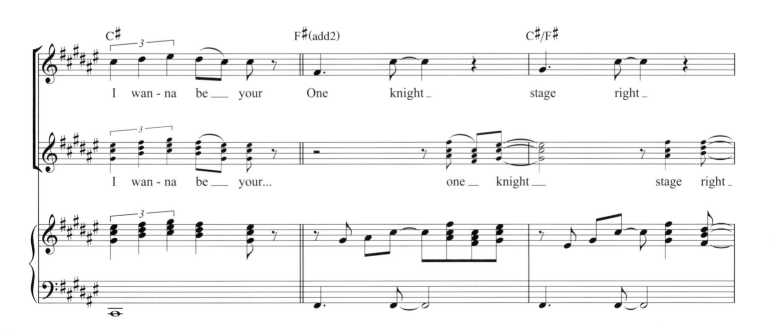

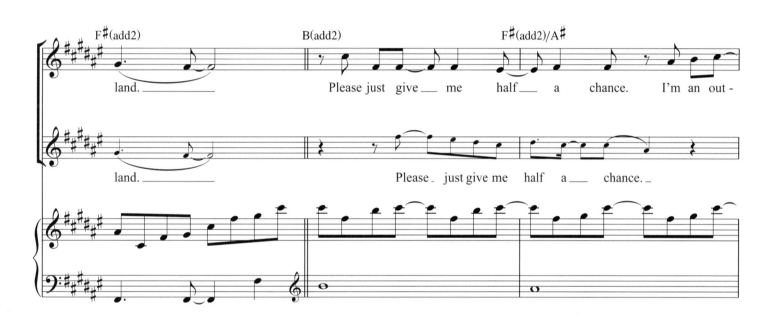

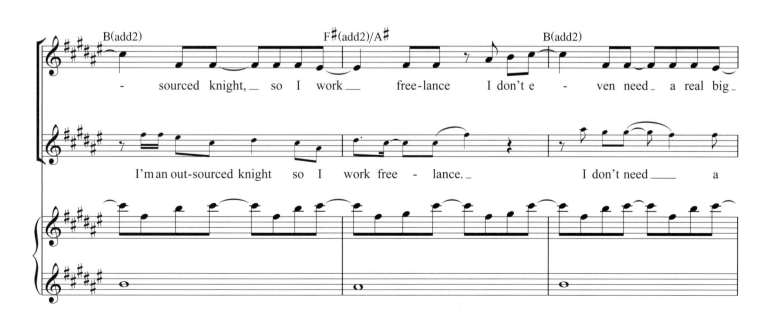

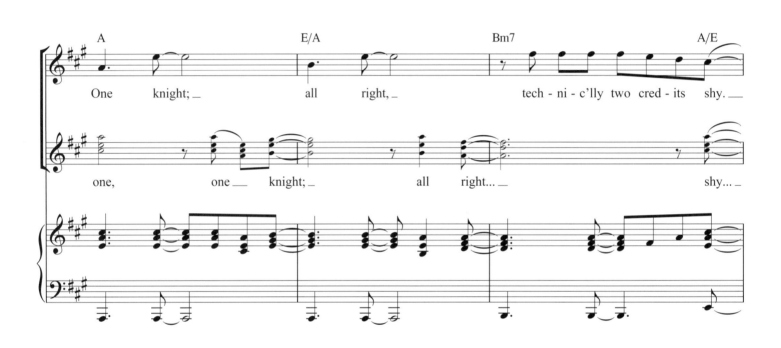

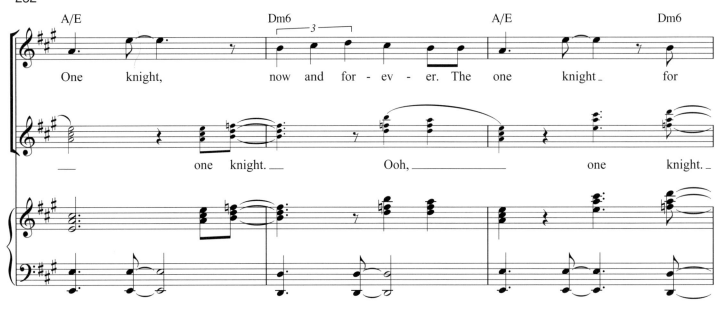

One knight, now and for - ev - er. The one knight _ for

one knight. _ Ooh, _ one knight. _

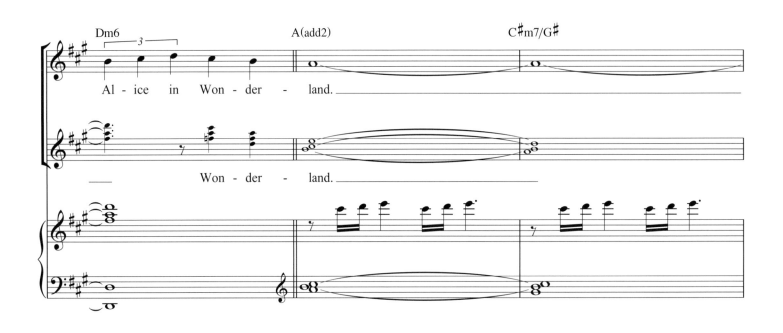

Al - ice in Won - der - land. _

Won - der - land. _

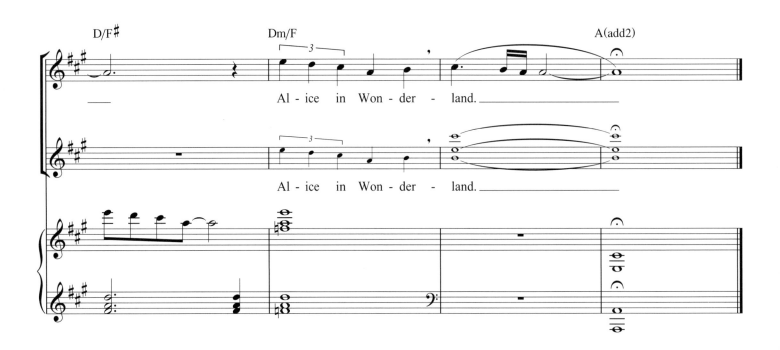

Al - ice in Won - der - land. _

Al - ice in Won - der - land. _